Dramatic Sketches In Divorce Recovery

Robert Alan Ward

CSS Publishing Company, Inc., Lima, Ohio

I0146558

To Dorothy DeLong, founder and head of Heart Healers
at Emmanuel Faith Community Church.
Thank you for believing in me, and for the privilege of serving with you.

Copyright © 2000 by
CSS Publishing Company, Inc.
Lima, Ohio

Scripture quotations are from the *New American Standard Bible,* © 1960, 1962, 1963, 1968, 1971, 1972, 1973, 1975, 1977 by The Lockman Foundation. Used by permission.

ISBN 0-7880-1341-6   PRINTED IN U.S.A.

The Purpose Of This Work

Few would dispute that the ugly word "divorce" has come increasingly into more common usage in our society today. Sometimes it happens to us whether we like it or not. Despite our best efforts the marriage fails. Are such individuals doomed to a life of ruin?

I firmly believe that any person who will cry out to God and obey Him through any adverse circumstance, will come through that situation better than before — divorce included. God's people are never in checkmate. Indeed, if we follow Christ, we always win (2 Corinthians 2:14). The first purpose of this work is to help those devastated by divorce to get through it and emerge triumphant, whether the marriage can be restored or not.

We want to help restore marriages wherever it can be done. And we want to help those marriages on the road to becoming what God intended them to be. There is more at stake than a broken marriage. There is the reputation of our Lord to consider. Then too, the process of reconciling a broken marriage inculcates the development of Christ-like character. The divorce decision is often an attempt to create more ideal circumstances without the effort of developing that character. Christians are called to Christ-likeness, not happiness. Such shortcuts to happiness will only lead to misery.

But more often than not, by the time people come to a divorce recovery group, it is too late. It is usually the individual who wanted to preserve the marriage that ends up in such a group. Such people need to be treated with compassion and sensitivity. Christians must not shoot their wounded. For those coming who do not know Christ, it is an optimum time for them to hear of the Savior.

If anyone is made to feel guilty or uncomfortable through these sketches, I pray that such guilt be only from the conviction of the Holy Spirit — no less, no more. The goal is not to induce guilt, but to bring about healing. If anyone feels that one gender is being favored over the other, I apologize. Neither sex is morally superior to the other. In actuality, without Christ, we are all morally bankrupt.

Some churches or other groups will want to develop divorce recovery programs, both for their own members, and as an outreach to the community around them. This work is intended to be a tool in helping to develop such a program. The ten subjects covered deal with issues that most people going through a divorce will have to face. The explanations of the subjects are intended to aid in the development of messages to be given after the dramas. The dramatic sketches are not intended necessarily to cover the entire subject of the week. Some do; others cover only one point under the broader subject. The questions and applications after each sketch are to stimulate discussion, perhaps after the message or in small group time.

May God richly bless your efforts to serve Him.

Robert Alan Ward

Table Of Contents

The Comforters

But as many as received Him, to them He gave the right to become children of God, to those who believe in His name....   — John 1:12

The divorce experience brings with it emotions of anger, guilt, worthlessness, humiliation, loneliness, desperation, and despair. In addition, the individual going through it will get advice (some good and some bad) from well-meaning people. How does one going through one of life's worst experiences navigate through the wilderness to solid ground?

This first sketch is meant to communicate the following to those who have come:

"You've made a good decision. You've come to the right place. Here we won't sing songs to troubled hearts (Proverbs 25:20), pronounce judgment upon you (Matthew 7:1-2), or take advantage of you in your present vulnerability (Matthew 27:35). Here you will have a chance to speak your heart in confidence with a group leader and others going through the same experience. Here you will get solid teaching on what to do about your situation and encouragement in doing those right things. Stick with us. We'll help you get through it."

My dear fellow ministers in divorce recovery: Deliver on those communications. Set your hearts to be men and women of God. Help those who have come to become whole again.

Characters:
Jane — the victim
David — the not-so-understanding husband
Sabrina — "don't worry, be happy"
Prudence — heaping on the guilt
Eddie — spend your troubles away

Setting: Jane's home. David is just returning from work.

David: I'm home, Jane. Food! (*He never looks at her, but uses the remote to turn on the television*)

Jane: David, would you please turn off the TV? (*He ignores her and keeps watching*) David, please turn off the TV. It's been a horrible day.

David: (*He turns it off and flips the remote aside in irritation*) All right — what?

Jane: Where do I start? A pipe burst under our bathroom sink. I called a plumber and he fixed the pipe, but the bill is $285 and our hallway floor is ruined. The school called to tell me that Billy was caught with drugs on campus. He's suspended for the rest of the year. Remember the guy who broke his ankle tripping over a backyard sprinkler while trying to steal our avocados last January? We got served with papers today. He's suing us for $100,000. Then Dr. Perkins called with the biopsy results on my tumor. It's malignant. He says they're working on a plan but the prognosis isn't good.

David: (*Gets up to leave*) Well, Jane, it's a rough life. See ya.

Jane: Where are you going?

David: God put me here to enjoy my life. How can I do that if I have to deal with all these hassles — and all the while watching you shrivel up and die? I don't think so. (*He exits*)

Jane: (*Hurtfully*) David ... (*The phone rings*) Hello.

Sabrina: Jane! The best thing just happened to me! I just won $50,000 in the lottery! I'm in seventh heaven. Should I get a Mercedes or a Beamer? What about redoing my kitchen?

Jane: I'm happy for you, Sabrina.

Sabrina: You don't sound very happy about it. How come?

Jane: It's been a rough day. I've had a couple of disasters here at home — Billy's into drugs, I'm being sued, I have cancer, and David just left me.

Sabrina: Don't worry. Be happy!

Jane: Huh?

Sabrina: Smile! Think happy thoughts. Sing a happy song. Here, I'll teach you one.

Jane: I don't feel much like singing right now, Sabrina.

Sabrina: Boy, you sure are a grouch!

(*She hangs up. The doorbell rings. Jane opens the door and Prudence enters, breathing fire*)

Prudence: Jane, I just ran into David down the street. How could you be so awful?

Jane: I don't know, Prudence.

Prudence: He told me about all the problems you've caused. There's only one conclusion, Jane — sin. You're living in sin. Bad things don't happen to good people.

8

Jane: I've always tried to live my life the way I feel God wants me to live it.

Prudence: And now you're lying. Repent, Jane. Repent, and all your problems will disappear. (*She looks at her watch*) Oh, gotta' run. Can't be late for the women's Bible study. I'll be praying for you to repent.

(*As she exits, she bumps into Eddie, who is just entering. She glares at him and is gone. Eddie comes in like he owns the place*)

Eddie: Janey, baby. It's your old friend, Eddie. Hear you're havin' a little trouble. I got just the thing for you. (*He hands Jane a brochure*)

Jane: What's this?

Eddie: The dream of a lifetime. A Hawaiian vacation package from my travel agency. You owe it to yourself.

Jane: I can't afford a Hawaiian vacation.

Eddie: Sure you can. You've got credit cards!

Jane: What about my children?

Eddie: It's time you started thinking about yourself. Hey, you never know. You might be at one of those banyan tree bars some night at Waikiki and some handsome hunk happens by — it could be a beautiful new beginning.

Jane: I don't know, Eddie.

Eddie: And if you act today, your cat flies free!

Jane: (*She shows him the door*) Well, thanks for your concern.

Eddie: This is a once-in-a-lifetime opportunity. (*She motions him out*) What about my commission?

(*She closes the door on him. She then picks up the phone and dials*)

Jane: Hello, (*name of your church*)? Do you have anything available for people going through hard times?

Questions to consider:

1. Have you had anyone give you the "Don't worry, be happy" approach?

2. Have you felt judged by others?

3. Has anyone tried to take advantage of you in your situation?

4. What would be the Christian response to any of the above scenarios?

Application for the week:

1. Begin a personal journal. In a large notebook begin to write down your thoughts, feelings, and experiences as you travel through your situation. How often you make entries is your decision. Try not to go more than one week between entries. Be sure to date every entry. This may become a lifelong habit. As the years go by, you will find it to be an increasingly valuable possession.

2. If anyone is treating you according to any of the above scenarios, pray about how you will respond. Find some Bible verses to help you respond God's way. Record all this in your journal. Record the results as well.

3. If you do not at this time have assurance of eternal life in Jesus Christ, consider this following explanation of how you can become a Christian.

    A. God loves you and wants you to be His child.
        For God so loved the world, that He gave His only begotten Son, that whoever believes in Him should not perish, but have eternal life (John 3:16).

    B. Your sin has separated you from God and His love.
        For all have sinned and fall short of the glory of God (Romans 3:23).

    C. Jesus Christ went to the cross to pay for your sins.
        And He Himself bore our sins in His body on the cross, that we might die to sin and live to righteousness; for by His wounds you were healed (1 Peter 2:24).

D. You must receive Jesus Christ by faith in order to become God's child and appropriate His gift to you of eternal life.
But as many as received Him, to them He gave the right to become children of God, to those who believe in His name ... (John 1:12).

E. How is eternal life in Jesus Christ possible? Because He arose from the dead.
And the angel answered and said to the woman, "Do not be afraid; for I know that you are looking for Jesus who has been crucified. He is not here, for He has risen, just as He said. Come, see the place where He was lying" (Matthew 28:5-6).

4. Just as Jesus arose from the dead, so too can your life arise from the ashes and become far more than you ever dreamed, if you will tie your life to His. The following is a suggested prayer for becoming a child of God. The exact words are less important than the real desire of your heart.

"Lord Jesus Christ, I need You. I know that I have sinned and deserve condemnation. But please have mercy on me. Please enter my life right now and make me into the person you want me to be. Thank you for dying on the cross for my sins and entering my life as you promised."

There is no more important or better decision in all of life than that of becoming God's child through Jesus Christ.

Which Voice?

We are destroying speculations and every lofty thing raised up against the knowledge of God, and we are taking every thought captive to the obedience of Christ...."

— 2 Corinthians 10:5

There are two kinds of guilt: real and false. A person going through divorce will often experience one or both. Either way, God has provided a way to deal with it. Real guilt will, for the Christian, bring with it the conviction of the Holy Spirit. This is painful, but it is healthy and necessary. We repent of our sin, appropriate the blood of Jesus Christ shed for us on the cross, and are restored to full fellowship with God. Real guilt is constructive if dealt with in God's way.

False guilt is destructive. It comes from not appropriating or believing in God's provision for our sin. Instead, we listen to the accusations of others or from the devil or his demons. The devil berates us (Revelation 12:10) with the idea of tearing us down. Any accusation coming at us from such a spirit is to be rejected. But in order to reject it effectively, we must counter the accusation with the truths of God (Ephesians 6:10-17).

The following sketch illustrates false guilt at work. Make sure the people understand the difference between real and false guilt so that they know what to accept and what to reject.

Characters:
The Victim
The Lie
The Truth

Scripture passages:

Jeremiah 31:3	2 Timothy 4:16-17
Romans 5:8	Luke 22:44
Isaiah 43:2, 4	Romans 8:31
Ezekiel 18:20	

Setting: The Truth sits offstage and out of sight, simply reading the Scripture passages at the appropriate times. The Lie is on stage and visible to the audience, but not to the Victim. The Lie enters, creeps up behind the Victim, and blows gently into her hair. The Victim becomes aware of the presence of evil.

The Lie: You are the ugliest, most despicable, rotten human being that ever lived. That's why your husband left you.

Victim: It's true. It's true.

The Truth: "I have loved you with an everlasting love." "But God demonstrates His own love toward us, in that while we were yet sinners, Christ died for us."

(Each time a passage is quoted, the Victim brightens up, while the Lie brings discouragement)

The Lie: You lost your job because you're worthless.

(The Victim picks up a Bible and sees this next passage)

The Truth: "When you pass through the waters, I will be with you; and through the rivers, they will not overflow you. When you walk through the fire, you will not be scorched, nor will the flame burn you ... since you are precious in My sight, since you are honored and I love you."

(The Lie pulls the Bible from the Victim's hands and sets it down on a table. The Lie never actually touches the Victim or the Bible, but his hands "pull" from a few inches away)

The Lie: Your children are mad at you because you're a bad parent.

The Truth: "The son will not bear the punishment for the father's iniquity, nor will the father bear the punishment for the son's iniquity."

The Lie: You have no friends. Nobody cares about you.

The Truth: "At my first defense no one supported me, but all deserted me ... But the Lord stood with me, and strengthened me."

The Lie: Look at your emotions. They're out of control. Christians are supposed to be in control. Are you sure you're a Christian? I don't think so. In fact, you aren't a Christian. You're a phony!

The Truth: "Jesus, being in agony ... was praying very fervently; and His sweat became like drops of blood, falling down upon the ground."

The Lie: You're hopeless.

The Victim: *(The Victim turns directly to the Lie and gets in his face)* That's enough of your lies. I choose to believe the truth. "If God is for me, who can be against me?"

(At this, the Lie is upset and steps back a couple of paces)

The Lie: There will be another time. *(The Lie exits)*

Questions to consider:

1. What are some other lies of the devil?

2. What is the difference between the conviction of the Holy Spirit and the berating of the devil?

3. What are some Bible verses that you have found helpful in your situation?

Application for the week:

1. Do you sit under the teaching of the word of God at least once a week?

2. Are you doing any personal intake of the word of God? If not, your group leader can help you get started.

3. Find some Scripture passages that you can adopt that deal directly with your situation and share them with the group next week.

To Grandmother's House

God is our refuge and strength, a very present help in trouble.   — Psalm 46:1

In addition to being an agony of the soul, divorce brings with it a myriad of often complicated issues (e.g. child custody, financial support, division of property, other broken relationships, and so forth) that must be dealt with. How does one cope with such issues while in so painful a state?

Many people attempt to avoid the issues altogether. But ignoring cancer seldom makes it go away. Others attempt to drown the problem with drugs, alcohol, new relationships, or spending sprees. Such answers usually only complicate the situation and diminish one's ability to deal with it.

God's approach is to face the problem squarely, using His wisdom and strength. It will be the most painful solution initially, but the least painful in the long run.

No matter how tough the circumstances we must face, we can rise above them when we avail ourselves to God.

Characters:
Grandmother
Little Miss Goldie Muffin Hood (LMGMH)
The Hungry Wolf

Setting: LMGMH is at stage right. Grandmother is opposite. The Wolf is in the middle. Grandmother calls LMGMH on the phone.

Grandmother: Hello, Little Miss Goldie Muffin Hood.

LMGMH: Grandmother! Oh, what a nice voice you have.

Grandmother: All the better to invite you to come over and help me bake cookies for (*name of your divorce recovery program*). You're the perfect little girl to make sure they're not too sweet, not too bland, but just right.

LMGMH: Goody! I'll be right over. (*She hangs up, puts on her red hood, picks up her basket, and heads out. In the middle she encounters the wolf*)

Wolf: Grooowl!

LMGMH: Hey, you're scaring me! That's very rude!

Wolf: It's all part of my act. What's in the basket, little girl?

LMGMH: Nothing. It's all part of my act, so that I look like the nice, sweet, wholesome, little girl that I am.

Wolf: Well, then, it's nothing personal, but I'm hungry. And since there's nothing in your basket, well ...

LMGMH: No! (*She runs back home and calls Grandmother*) Grandmother? I can't make it today. There's a big, mean, hungry wolf on the path that wants to eat me up!

Grandmother: Oh, him. Listen, Little Miss Goldie Muffin Hood. Put on your gold sweater and take along your wolfbeater's club that I gave you last Christmas. If he bugs you again, blast him.

LMGMH: But, Grandmother, he has big, sharp teeth!

Grandmother: Then knock them out with your club. Come on, Little Miss Goldie Muffin Hood. We've got cookies to bake.

LMGMH: Well, all right. But I'm still scared. (*She hangs up the phone, puts on her gold sweater, picks up her wolfbeater's club, and heads out. She encounters the Wolf*)

Wolf: Grooowl!

LMGMH: Please, Mr. Wolf. I have to get to Grandmother's house.

Wolf: Yeah, well, you might just end up real late. (*Laughs at his joke*) How come you're wearing that gold sweater? It's awfully hot out today.

LMGMH: (*Getting bolder*) Glad you don't like it. Now stand aside. I have urgent cookie business to tend to.

Wolf: You haven't caught on to my drift, have you?

(*LMGMH rolls her eyes and then hits Wolf with her club*)

Wolf: (*Yelps like an injured dog*) Why did you have to do that? I'm just a nice wolfy in need of a meal.

LMGMH: Hey, I'm sorry, but life is tough all over. There's some nice grass over there. Eat that. I gotta go now. (*She waves good-bye*)

(*Wolf sits down and pouts. LMGMH gets to Grandmother's house*)

LMGMH: Hi, Grandmother. Like my gold sweater? I whacked the wolf like you said, and he wasn't nearly as scary after that.

Grandmother: Excellent. After all that, you need a good carbohydrate. How about some porridge?

LMGMH: Let's cut straight to the cookies.

Grandmother: That's my Little Miss Goldie Muffin Hood.

(*They exit*)

Questions to consider:

1. What are some wrong ways we often choose to deal with our problems?

2. What are the advantages to be gained by facing our problems God's way?

3. If God's way is better, why do we sometimes choose our way?

Application for the week:

1. Choose *one* issue that you must deal with (whether you like it or not). Define the issue completely on paper. Go before God and pray about how you ought to tackle it. Ask God for the right heart to deal with it. Search the Scriptures. Consult a godly friend and get his or her input. Write down your findings on the same paper. Do what you have written and record the results (as far as they have gone as of your writing). Share the process with the group next week and request their prayers.

The Lone Parent

And if one member suffers, all the members suffer with it ...   — 1 Corinthians 12:26

There ought to be no such thing as a "free agent" Christian. God's people are meant to work together as do the parts of the human body (1 Corinthians 12:12-21). But what if a member of Christ's body is hurting? That is one reason why the church exists.

When a need is known, God's people usually rally to the aid of the needy one. The other side is that those who hurt need to communicate their need. If for no other reason, they need to realize that their pain hurts everyone else.

The humility such an admission requires is good for the hurting one. So is the opportunity for another to be blessed by giving. And maybe the need is so great that one just can't make it without help. So if you're down and need help, get it. Maybe later you'll be able to help someone else.

Characters:
Mom
Franklin — Twelve-year-old son
Tilly — Ten-year-old daughter
Biscuit — Six-year-old daughter

Mom: (*On the phone*) No, I'm managing fine, Hortense. (*Listens*) Of course. I'll call you if I need help. 'Bye. (*Hangs up*)

Franklin: Mom, I need you to sign this permission slip for me to go on the environmental awareness field trip at school.

Mom: All right. (*She starts to sign and then notices the fine print*) Hey, wait a minute. Twenty-five dollars for the insurance fee?

Franklin: That's in case we accidentally harm an endangered species.

Mom: Franklin, I don't have $25 to spare.

Franklin: But, Mom, everybody's going. They'll be having a blast while I have to stay in class and write a paper on cultural diversity.

Mom: (*Sighing*) All right, I suppose we can squeeze somewhere else. Go get my checkbook.

(*Franklin exits; Biscuit enters*)

Biscuit: Mom, Tilly's got Tiggy! She says she's going to tie her to the railroad tracks!

Mom: Tilly, give Biscuit back her doll.

(*Enter Tilly*)

Tilly: I don't have Tiggy. The police took her away because she wet her bed.

Biscuit: Mom, call the police. Make them bring Tiggy back!

Mom: Tilly, that's enough. Go get Tiggy this instant!

(*Exit Tilly; enter Franklin, who trips Tilly as they pass*)

Franklin: (*Hands Mom the checkbook*) Uh, Mom. The toilet just overflowed.

Mom: What did you do to it?

Franklin: I did everything the way I always do it.

Mom: Go get the plunger.

Franklin: Umm ... we don't have a plunger anymore.

Mom: What?!

Franklin: I needed the rubber part for a school project.

(*Enter Tilly*)

Tilly: Mom, I think Tiggy might be stuck in the toilet.

Mom: Ahhhh! You kids! How am I ever supposed to raise you by myself?

Tilly: We're basically good kids.

Mom: (*Without a lot of conviction*) Right.

Franklin: Didn't Hortense ask you to call if you need help? Her husband is a plumber.

Mom: I can't be bothering other people with my problems.

Franklin: Mr. Finklehauser told us in Sunday school that all of us need help sometimes.

(*Phone rings*)

Mom: Hello? (*Listens. Her countenance completely changes to reflect a sunny disposition*) Oh, fine, Alice. Things couldn't be better. How's Chuck?

(*The children look at one another in amazement and exit together one way*)

Mom: That's great. I gotta' go, Alice. It's time for me to read to my children before bed. (*Listens*) My secret? Just prayer. (*Listens*) All right. 'Bye.

(*She hangs up. Her countenance drops again as she exits the other way*)

Questions to consider:

1. Why are some people so reluctant to ask for help?

2. What are some things we do to hide our real needs? Consider emotional, physical, financial, and spiritual.

3. What is the balance between asking for too little or too much help?

4. What kinds of help do single parents need?

Application for the week:

1. Ask someone capable to help you with a need that you cannot meet yourself.

2. Are there any areas in which you are getting help, but now can handle for yourself? How will you wean yourself from it?

The Creditors

And my God shall supply all your needs according to His riches in glory in Christ Jesus.
— Philippians 4:19

Among other things, divorce brings financial hardship. Two households have to be maintained. Money is eaten up in lawyers' fees. Sometimes we react to trauma by rashly overspending.

So what do we do about it? There are two factors in finances. The first is how much we make; the second is how we use it. One who knows how to handle money properly can make little seem like much more.

How? Purchasing only necessities; used is often as good as new; sales and coupons; creative entertainment; learning skills yourself; planning; and get the children earning. Here is a good credo to live by: "Use it up. Wear it out. Make it do, or do without."

If you have done all you can and still lack, the church may be able to help. Most churches have funds for those who are trying their best and just need a little more to get over the top. Individuals in the church might be available for plumbing emergencies or other maintenance.

Finally, we can believe God. "I have been young," said David, "and now I am old; yet I have not seen the righteous forsaken, or his descendants begging bread" (Psalm 37:25).

Characters:
Mom
Eight Creditors
Daughter

(*Enter Mom. She is wearing a fancy hat and carrying a purse and a bag of groceries. In the hand of the purse-carrying arm is a wad of money*)

Mom: At last — a paycheck! Is it ever good to get money in my hands! (*She kisses her money*)

First Creditor: (*He enters and holds out his hand*) House payment!

(*She gives him some dollars. He exits. Enter Second Creditor as first leaves*)

Second Creditor: Car payment!

(She gives him some dollars. He exits. Then in rapid succession, six more creditors enter from every direction and surround her, holding out their hands and shouting their demands over and over)

Third Creditor: Phone bill!

Fourth Creditor: Gas bill!

Fifth Creditor: Orthodontics bill!

Sixth Creditor: Lawyer's fees!

Seventh Creditor: Charge cards!

Eighth Creditor: Taxes!

(She gives each money until it runs out. The Sixth Creditor takes her hat right off her head. The Seventh Creditor yanks away her purse. The Eighth Creditor takes her grocery bag. All exit and leave her standing there desolate. Enter Daughter)

Daughter: Mom, I need money to buy clothes for school.

(Mom says nothing, but with a sad look on her face, she puts her arm around her daughter and together they exit)

Questions to consider:

1. What are some extra expenses incurred by those going through divorce?

2. What are some possible ways of increasing income?

3. What are some possible ways of decreasing expenses?

4. Should a single parent who is financially struggling stop giving?

5. What are some good financial habits?

Application for the week:

1. Make up a budget by which you can track your entire income and every expenditure for a month. See where your money is going. Set yourself goals for the next month, and for the year.

2. Begin a savings program.

3. Pray and write down ways you can ease your economic situation without sacrificing too much time from your children (e.g., selling unneeded material things, a part-time job, a home job, coupons, creative entertainment, doing without and so on).

Spouse Bashing

Do not speak against one another, brethren. He who speaks against a brother, or judges his brother, speaks against the law, and judges the law; but if you judge the law, you are not a doer of the law, but a judge of it.   — James 4:11

Divorce is hard on all parties concerned. If children are involved, they will suffer at least as much as their parents through no fault of their own. There are, however, things parents can do that will help keep a bad situation from getting worse. Children do not enjoy being spies for one or the other parent. They do not wish to be caught between parents in the "no man's land" of a custody battle, or in financial disputes. Most of all, they don't want to hear each parent demonize the other.

Characters:
Orville — Father
Gretta — Mother
Courtney — Daughter

Setting: Courtney comes into the house in front of her dad. Both arms are laden with Disney paraphernalia and she is wearing a Mickey Mouse hat.

Courtney: Thanks for taking me to Disneyland, Dad.

Orville: Anything for my sweet Courtney.

Gretta: Do you have my support check, Orville?

Orville: Yeah, I got it, Gretta. Here, I'll air mail it to you. (*He throws it at her as a glider*)

Gretta: Disrespectful as usual. Hit the road, you toad.

Orville: You got it, lame lips. (*He exits*)

Gretta: What did I ever see in that man? Out of the ten worst decisions I ever made, the top nine were marrying him.

Courtney: (*Irritated*) Mom ...

29

Gretta: He is living proof that at least some humans really did evolve from slime.

Courtney: (*More irritated*) Mom ...

Gretta: I'd love to will his brain to science. Maybe they could find a cure for warped minds like his.

Courtney: Mom ... (*More irritated still. She heads over to get the whistle*)

Gretta: And have you noticed that beer belly forming around his flabby gut?

(*Courtney blows the whistle*)

Courtney: Time out! Time out! I don't want to hear any more.

Gretta: Whose side are you on?

Courtney: Neither. I won't let him bad mouth you either.

Gretta: There's nothing bad to tell.

Courtney: Mom, you say it's his fault. He says it's your fault. Maybe it was my fault. I hate this whole thing. (*She starts to cry*)

Gretta: It wasn't your fault, Courtney.

Courtney: Mom, you both taught me that the Bible says to honor my father and my mother. How can I do that when you keep slamming each other?

Gretta: You're right, honey. (*Repentant*) I'm sorry.

Courtney: It's okay, Mom. (*They hug*)

Questions to consider:

1. How does hearing one parent slam the other hurt a child?

2. How should you respond if the other parent has spoken ill of you to your children?

3. What are some good things you might be able to tell your children about your former partner?

4. Is there ever a time when it *is* necessary to speak negative things about the other parent?

Application for the week:

1. What are some positive, constructive things you can do or say that will relieve tension in your children's lives?

2. What are some Bible verses you can memorize and claim to help you with your tongue? (e.g., Psalm 141:3; Psalm 39:1; James 3:2)

3. Is there anyone to whom you need to apologize?

The Boss

For you who judge practice the same things.   — Romans 2:1b

Forgiveness and repentance are two sides of the same basic issue. In the sketch given here, Mr. Harris can readily see the sins of his wife (which are real) but has no clue that he does the same thing. How is this possible? It is because the human "heart is more deceitful than all else and is desperately sick; who can understand it?" (Jeremiah 17:9). I am convinced that the root of divorce lies in our human tendency to condemn others for their shortcomings while not realizing that we do the same things ourselves.

So what is the solution? It is to go before God in all honesty and confess our own sins, not our spouse's. How do we know our own sins? Hebrews 4:12-13 tells us that the word of God is "able to judge the thoughts and intentions of the heart. And there is no creature hidden from His sight, but all things are open and laid bare to the eyes of Him with whom we have to do." We cannot fool God, and "If we say that we have no sin, we are deceiving ourselves, and the truth is not in us" (1 John 1:8). The Holy Spirit convicts us of sin (John 16:8). If we will be honest before God and heed His word, the Holy Spirit will show us our sin.

Psalm 51 is the great Psalm of repentance. David had committed adultery with Bathsheba and then murdered her husband to cover his sin. When confronted, he repented. Psalm 51 shows his heart. He could have blamed Bathsheba. After all, she was the one who was bathing. She came willingly. She didn't tell Uriah what was up. But none of those factors took David off the hook. "The thing that David had done was evil in the sight of the Lord" (2 Samuel 11:27).

But when David was honest before God and took full responsibility for his actions, God gave grace. There is no other spirit that God loves more than a repentant spirit. Those who will be honest before God receive an overflowing abundance of grace. We don't deserve it, but there it is.

And now comes the forgiveness side of the issue. When we have been honest with God and received His grace, our spirits respond gratefully toward Him and graciously toward others. We look upon the sins of others not with condemnation, but with sorrow for how it breaks God's heart and how it is harming their souls and other people. Our spirits yearn for the other party to be set free. We forgive even if the other person sees no need of it. Show me a man who cannot forgive, and I will show you a man who has not learned God's grace for his own sins.

If both husband and wife possess such grateful spirits, divorce cannot happen. If only one will go this route, God will give grace for that individual to endure and will do a great work in his or her life.

Characters:
Mr. Harris
Employee
Counselor

Setting: Mr. Harris is sitting at his executive desk looking over some papers. Enter Employee from stage right.

Employee: You called for me, Mr. Harris?

Harris: Yes, I've been going over your fitness reports, and I'm sorry to say that your performance is unsatisfactory. You are hereby terminated.

Employee: But, Mr. Harris. I've been doing my best. Everybody tells me I'm improving.

Harris: Not fast enough, I'm afraid.

Employee: Please, Mr. Harris. I'm a single mom. This is a hard time in my life. I need this job.

Harris: This is a business, not a charity.

Employee: I've been here nearly twenty years. I'm only six months away from qualifying for retirement.

Harris: What can I say? Life is hard and we have to cut costs. Clean out your locker. You can pick up your last paycheck next Friday. Good day.

(*Employee exits. Harris moves to stage left and sits opposite his marriage counselor*)

Harris: I don't understand how my wife can be so unfeeling.

Counselor: How has she been unfeeling, Henry?

Harris: She said I just wasn't changing fast enough. Hey, I was doing my best. She has no idea of the pressure I'm under at work.

Counselor: Have you told her about the pressure you're under at work?

Harris: She doesn't care. She says she can't do anything about that, and that it's no excuse for me not being the kind of husband I ought to be. It's like there's no concern about me as a person. It's all about what I do or don't do for her.

Counselor: I'll discuss that with her next time she comes in.

Harris: Do that. I can't understand how some people can be so cruel.

Questions to consider:

1. Why is it easier to see another person's faults rather than our own?

2. What is the root of an unforgiving spirit?

3. How does one develop a forgiving spirit?

4. Why is a forgiving spirit essential to one's spiritual, mental, and physical health?

Application for the week:

1. List the things you feel that you did (or didn't do) that contributed to the failure of your marriage.

2. Go before God with that list and confess your failures to Him. Accept His grace and forgiveness (1 John 1:9).

3. If appropriate, ask your former spouse's forgiveness for those failures, *without* bringing up where you think he or she failed.

   (Note: In asking forgiveness, be careful about submitting a written confession. "Be ye therefore wise as serpents, and harmless as doves" (Matthew 10:16, KJV). Written confessions can be shown to others who have no need to know about them, or even wind up in a courtroom as evidence against you.)

The Dart Game

*Therefore if any man is in Christ, he is a new creature, the old things passed away; behold,
new things have come. Now all these things are from God, who reconciled us to Himself
through Christ, and gave us the ministry of reconciliation, namely, that God was in Christ
reconciling the world to Himself, not counting their trespasses against them, and He has
committed to us the word of reconciliation.* — 2 Corinthians 5:17-19

The Scriptures are full of accounts of reconciliation. One of the best known is the parable of the prodigal son (Luke 15:11-32). Indeed, the whole plan of God toward humankind is one of an initial relationship (the Garden of Eden), the fall, and the reconciliation through Christ's sacrifice on the cross. The very essence of the Christian life is forgiveness and reconciliation.

In a broken marriage, reconciliation involves two aspects: forgiveness and trust. Forgiveness is given. Trust is earned. If a marriage is broken because of adultery, for instance, the offender may sincerely repent and ask forgiveness of the other spouse. The offended is obligated before God to forgive the offender, but not necessarily to resume the marriage. The offender must regain the other's trust over a period of time, and consider it grace if the offended ever agrees to trust again. The offender has no more right to demand reinstatement than any of us have to demand salvation.

Sometimes, each party has greatly wounded the other. In such cases reconciliation would better take the form, not of the father to the prodigal son, but of two prodigals coming together. Such an occurrence is indispensable; but it is only the beginning of a restored marriage. The parties ought to remain separated and give themselves time to rebuild trust slowly and kindle afresh the flame of romance. The process will bring about great development of character. The result will be a marriage far better than the original.

Reconciliation may not always result in a restored marriage. Sometimes circumstances (e.g., one of the spouses has remarried) make it impossible. Yet reconciliation is still a desirable thing. Perhaps the former couple will stop being enemies and learn to cooperate. Even though the marriage cannot be restored, each will find a clearer passageway to fellowship with God, and some of the negative consequences from their divorce will diminish.

Finally, reconciliation is not imperative for one spouse to enjoy unrestricted fellowship with God. If one spouse wants to make things right, but the other is unwilling, the former's ability to walk with God is not held hostage to the latter's unwillingness.

Characters:
Mom
Jerusha — Daughter

(*Mom is throwing darts at a picture of her ex-husband*)

Mom: Rats! Why can't I hit him in the eye? (*Enter Jerusha*)

Jerusha: What are you doing, Mom?

Mom: Playing darts, Jerusha.

Jerusha: Hey, that's a picture of Dad.

Mom: That's the idea. I thought it might help motivate me to improve my aim.

Jerusha: (*Goes over and takes the picture down*) Mom, I don't want you doing this. It's time you gave it up.

Mom: After what he did?

Jerusha: Mom, can't you see how sorry he is? Ever since that time, he's been a good man. He's made his support payments. And how do you think the plumbing got fixed last week?

Mom: He did it?

Jerusha: And asked me not to tell you. He said he doesn't deserve your forgiveness.

Mom: That's the first thing he's said in a long time that I agree with.

Jerusha: Mom, haven't you ever done anything really bad?

Mom: (*Pauses to think*) Yeah, I guess I have.

Jerusha: I hate this divorce. I miss the vacations we used to have together. I miss the mealtimes. Remember when Dad used to read to us at night? And I miss my sister and brother. Can't anything be done?

Mom: I don't know.

Questions to consider:

1. What are some reasons one might be unwilling to reconcile with a former spouse?

2. What are the advantages of reconciliation?

3. Does reconciliation always result in a restored marriage?

4. If a marriage cannot be restored, is reconciliation still desirable?

Application for the week:

1. Is there any possibility of resurrecting your marriage?

2. If the answer is "yes," what will you begin to do now to help bring that about?

3. If the answer is "no," is there anything you can do to help bring about reconciliation (without restoring the marriage) anyway. (In some extreme cases, no attempt to contact the other party is the best course.)

    (Note: There is a line that I like to call "The Line of Reconciliation." When both parties come to that line, reconciliation can occur. If one party comes to the line, but the other will not, there is no reconciliation. There is, however, freedom for the willing party to enjoy full fellowship with God, to heal, and to go on to a fully productive life. "The Line of Reconciliation" is not a position of bondage, but of freedom.)

Injured

He who makes haste with his feet errs.   — Proverbs 19:2

Perhaps restoration of a marriage has become an impossibility. Is one therefore compelled to spend the rest of his or her life alone? The Scriptures give permission for one who has lost a spouse through death to remarry (Romans 7:1-3). Jesus seems to have implied that one who divorces an adulterous spouse has permission to remarry (Matthew 5:31-32). A third situation might be termed "desertion by an unbelieving spouse" (1 Corinthians 7:15). "The brother or the sister is not under bondage in such cases...." I take that to mean that there is permission to remarry after it has become evident that the unbelieving spouse is not coming back.

Beyond these exceptions I am personally afraid to venture. Let each individual make up his or her own mind on this issue, and take full responsibility before God for any decision to remarry.

But in any scenario, it is wise to take one's time before committing to a lifelong relationship. In time, as we follow God's leading through a tough situation, we heal. With healing comes better judgment through a diminished sense of urgency. Single life can be a great blessing that allows us to pour our creative energies into other legitimate and fulfilling pursuits.

Above all, we must not get into a pattern of thinking that we can freely jettison a marriage any time the going gets a little rough and go find someone else. Such thinking will only bring about greater and greater heartache.

Characters:
Coach
Baker — wrapped up like he has a dozen injuries; and on crutches

Setting: Coach is seated at a desk going over some paperwork. He has a whistle around his neck. Baker enters from stage right.

Baker: Coach, can I talk to you for a second?

Coach: Sure, Baker. What is it?

Baker: I noticed my name isn't on the roster for tomorrow night's game. How come?

Coach: Baker, don't you remember? You were driven off the field in an ambulance last week. You have a broken leg, six broken ribs, a concussion, and internal injuries. You needed four pints of blood at the hospital. You're hurt. That's why you're not suiting.

Baker: But I'm practically 100 percent now. By tomorrow I'll be ready.

Coach: I can't put you out there. First of all, you'd be no good to us. You can hardly move. Secondly, if I let you play in the condition you're in, you'll be riding off this time in a hearse. Let me talk to you man to man, Baker. You're out for the season — maybe forever. There are other things in life besides football.

Baker: Don't tell me that. I can't live without football!

Coach: Can't life without football, huh? All right, I'll tell you what. Take this play book home and study it. You're a good football player, Baker, but the weakest part of your game has been not knowing this book. That's how you got blind-sided last Friday night. Let your body mend while you're studying. If you can get your doctor's clearance, come see me next August. I'll give you every chance to remake this team. Fair enough?

Baker: All right, Coach. Thanks for giving me something to shoot for. See you next August.

(*Baker exits*)

Questions to consider:

1. How is it that Baker was so oblivious to his injuries? Is it possible that one going through divorce might not realize how badly he is hurt or how poor his judgment is?

2. What are some other reasons that rushing into a new relationship on the heels of a divorce might be a bad idea?

3. What are some ways of safeguarding yourself when you think you are ready and have found a possible new mate?

4. What are some good policies in pursuing a new relationship? (e.g., no dating if still legally married, date only believers, abstinence from sex until marriage, and so on)

Application for the week:

1. Are you in a new relationship now and questioning the rightness of it? What are you going to do about it?

2. Write down some solid biblically-based policies regarding your own life and how you will or won't go about a new relationship. Pray them through and find a trusted friend of the same sex to hold you accountable to them.

The Cauldron

But He knows the way I take; when He has tried me, I shall come forth as gold.

— Job 23:10

Life is as unpredictable as the weather. We live a daily routine, and then suddenly we get hit with something totally unexpected. Nancy Kerrigan asked it best: "Why me?" A sudden illness, an accident, a financial reversal, the loss of a job, or a child, or a mate — in one way or another, heartache will eventually come to all of us.

Pain is part of the curse that came upon humankind when Adam, the father of us all, chose to disobey God (Genesis 3:17-19). But is sorrow really such a bad thing? Does it not serve a greater purpose if we deal with it God's way?

Pain will measure for us the extent to which our affections are rooted in this world or in God's kingdom. Equal disasters may strike two people, but one will weather the storm while the other will be swept away (Matthew 7:24-27). Understanding that truth, we know that although we cannot predict what may befall us, we can best prepare for hardship by rooting our lives in Jesus Christ. A man seeking God's kingdom will not feel so great a loss as the man whose entire affection is for this world.

Pain also has a cleansing effect on our lives (1 Peter 4:1-2) and helps serve to refocus our priorities toward God. That is the main point of this week's lesson. Divorce is not a good thing. But the person who will lean into the pain and discover God's grace, wisdom, love, and strength in dealing with it will emerge as one refined by the fire. All of us have God-given talent in some way, but few of us have character. Divorce is an excellent opportunity to learn character, which is infinitely more important than talent. Talent is useful for God's kingdom only when it is first based on character.

Characters:
Celebrity Starr
Gatekeeper
(Both roles can be of either gender)

Setting: The Gatekeeper is seated at a desk. Celebrity Starr enters carrying some cardstock signs, large enough to be read by the audience, and walks up to him at his desk. A sign (TO THE CAULDRON) with an arrow pointing beyond the desk to another exit is visible.

Celebrity Starr: I'm joining the Overcomers. Where do I sign? (*He grabs a pen and waits for the Gatekeeper to produce the proper paper*)

Gatekeeper: Hold on. Not just anybody can be an Overcomer.

Celebrity Starr: I can. The name's Celebrity Starr, and I've got it all. I'm buff — see. (*Holds up the "buff" sign for the Gatekeeper and audience to see*) Quite a stud, ain't I? And I'm smart. (*Holds up the "smart" sign*) Give me two, three-digit numbers, and I'll instantly tell you their product.

Gatekeeper: 113 times 537. (*Gets out his calculator and begins to punch it in*)

Celebrity Starr: 60,681.

Gatekeeper: (*Finishes punching it*) Very impressive.

Celebrity Starr: And I've got charm (*Holds up "charm" sign*), and I'm rich (*Holds up "rich" sign*), and I'm eloquent (*Holds up a sign that says "I talk good"*), and ...

Gatekeeper: So you feel like you're God's gift to the Overcomers.

Celebrity Starr: That about sums it up. You know, I've watched some of your people in action. Not a one has anything near my talent.

Gatekeeper: Maybe not, but they do have something else you might lack.

Celebrity Starr: What would that be?

Gatekeeper: Character.

Celebrity Starr: Character? What's that?

Gatekeeper: Character is strength born of conviction. It is having core values based on God's laws that are unnegotiable in the events of everyday life. It is making decisions based on purpose above pleasure — the permanent before the expedient. It is what makes you the kind of person that others can depend on to speak what is true and do what is right. It is loving others, especially when they don't deserve it. It is putting others ahead of yourself, and God first of all. Such a man is an Overcomer.

Celebrity Starr: So where do I get it?

Gatekeeper: There are several ways, but the fastest is to go through the Cauldron.

Celebrity Starr: What's the Cauldron?

Gatekeeper: It's different for everyone, and fun for no one.

Celebrity Starr: What would I want to do that for?

Gatekeeper: You said you wanted to be an Overcomer.

Celebrity Starr: So I did. Well, which way do I go?

Gatekeeper: That way. (*Points in the direction of the arrow. Celebrity Starr picks up his cards*) You won't be needing those.

Celebrity Starr: Why not?

Gatekeeper: In the Cauldron, they won't help you. They might even work against you.

Celebrity Starr: How can I make it through without all my talents?

Gatekeeper: Good question. That's where character comes in. You have to need it before you can develop it. And talent at your stage will only serve to make you think you don't need character.

(*At this, Celebrity Starr ponders for a moment. Then he quietly puts down his cards and enters into the Cauldron*)

Questions to consider:

1. What is the difference between talent and character?

2. Which of the two usually gives the more favorable first impression?

3. Is it true that talent, in order to be truly useful, must be based first on character? Defend your assertion.

4. What are some factors that might help encourage us to make right, rather than easy, choices regarding our circumstances?

Application for the week:

1. Write in your journal what you have done in the process of your divorce. Make two columns. On one side write, "What I have done right"; on the other, "What I have done wrong." Rejoice in what you have done right. Thank God for giving you the strength to do them. Confess your failures to God. It's all forgivable. Take one of them and pray about what you can do now to make it right. Write in your journal what you will do. Record the results when they occur. Results don't necessarily have to bring favorable reactions from others. Even more important is what doing right will do in you. After tackling the first wrong, you may be encouraged to go after the others.

2. Determine before God that you are going to survive this ordeal. No matter what, you are going to do what you know you ought to do. Record your affirmation in your journal.

www.ingramcontent.com/pod-product-compliance
Lightning Source LLC
Chambersburg PA
CBHW05035710O426
42739CB00015BB/3429